THE MUSIC SPACE

THE MUSIC SPACE

poems

April 10 – September 16, 2001

Daniel Abdal-Hayy Moore

The Ecstatic Exchange

2007

Philadelphia

The Music Space
Copyright © 2007 Daniel Abdal-Hayy Moore

Printed in the United States of America

For quotes any longer than those for critical articles and reviews, contact:
The Ecstatic Exchange,
6470 Morris Park Road, Philadelphia, PA 19151-2403
email: abdalhayy@danielmoorepoetry.com

First Edition
ISBN: 978-0-6151-5116-8 (paper)
Published by *The Ecstatic Exchange*,
6470 Morris Park Road, Philadelphia, PA 19151-240

Cover and text design by Abdallateef Whiteman / www.ianwhiteman.com
Cover collage by the author
Back cover photograph by Mukhtar Sanders

A Little Ramshackle Shack first appeared in the anthology
An Eye for an Eye Makes the Whole World Blind
edited by Allen Cohen & Clive Matson, 2002

بس ــــــــــــــــــــــــــــــ

CONTENTS

A NOTE ON THESE POEMS

PREPARING THIS COLLECTION FOR publication, I notice that this is more of a New York book than I had imagined. Many of the middle poems were written while I was working on dance narrative presentations (*The New York Ramayana*, and *Eagle Spirit: A Tribute to Native High Steel Workers*) for *Lotus Music & Dance*, the teaching and production studio of old friend, Kamela Cesar, formerly of my late 60s Berkeley ritual theater company, *The Floating Lotus Magic Opera Company*. She and her husband, baritone contemporary singer, Tom Buckner, hosted me for weeks at a time at their Manhattan penthouse. Never having spent any length of time in New York previously, I happily soaked up the Big Apple world of art and rapid transit, noise and actual music, recorded in my usual fashion in the ongoing manuscript of that time, this present volume, *The Music Space.*

What none of us could possibly have foreseen was the event that triggered its concluding poem, *The Little Ramshackle Shack*, which I began reluctantly, after the Twin Towers tragedy of September 11th, too troubled by its occurrence and its possible consequences to write a glib poem, and resisting it. What came, however, drove the music space theme of the book into a new dimension… and New York and the entire world have never sounded quite the same.

But I emerged from the heady ferment of the 60s (and in Berkeley, California!), and the "apocalyptic" was the current and even most natural mode of our existence then, which somehow makes todays' events (2007) utterly and supremely within a prevailing texture of apocalyptic consciousness. Everything was going to topple – those on high would be brought low, and the low ones would inherit the earth. We all seemed to see a fiery end to all things American, not through our own "revolutionary" efforts, but simply as the result of our country's, culture's and civilization's overwhelming arrogance, pride and increasingly incredible corporate attempts at world control: the Vietnam War, and for us today, the Iraq debacle. With Ginsberg's Moloch howling in our ears, some made the best of things by inner adventures, others by political action, in vain or not. Today, some belabor a continuation of the psychedelic philosophy of that "bygone era," while others, like myself, felt the next "revolutionary" step was a traditional spiritual Path. Many, I fear, just gave up.

But:

> *This is the music space*
> *where music is most difficult*
> *this place of joy and horror…*
>
> *I think the music of the spheres*
> *can be heard in this space…*
>
> *And the original sound is the*
> *sound of God alone audible to Himself*
>
> *and we are the humming elements of that sound…*

Music does not give rise, in the heart, to anything which is not already there: so he whose inner self is attached to anything else than God is stirred by music to sensual desire, but the one who is inwardly attached to the love of God is moved, by hearing music, to do His will…

The common folk listen to music according to nature, and the novices listen with desire and awe, while the listening of the saints brings them a vision of the Divine gifts and graces, and these are the gnostics to whom listening means contemplation. But finally, there is the listening of the spiritually perfect, to whom, through music, God reveals Himself unveiled.

— SHIHAB AL-DIN ABU HAFS AL-SUHRAWARDI

We rarely hear the inward music, but we're all dancing to it nevertheless.

— MAULANA RUMI

In my city one wished me death,
Nevermind,
The stars last more than one night –

— LOUIS ZUKOFSKY (A)

I   A VERY PRETTY SYMPHONY

A very pretty symphony played on only the
blue notes

watery streams in between
with enough grandeur to go around and for

everyone to walk around in comfortably
encapsulating and even embodying

the sound that grows between the
grassblades in that furtive vertical space where

bison herds have disappeared between the
greenest sheathes and

angels' faces flash and fade
but float forward in turquoise cloud for just

long enough for the music to be heard

4/10

2   MUSIC OF A SMALL SHREDDER

Music of a small shredder
music of a giant turbine mulching logs
music of a spoon hitting the edge of a salad bowl as it serves
these musics that a million birds might make

Music of her speech upstairs on the telephone to our son
wisps of airy melodious nothingness of the water heater's pilot light
or the watery flush moving through metal pipes in the house somewhere
distant tunes a few streets away music

Undulant airwaves of different decibels but actually at-this-moment
inaudible music
music of the heart speaking nothing but the truth
awful cacophony of untruths like the social Muzak that accompanies us
up elevator down

High clear notes from earth's horizon to the clouds
the behind-all-things visible to the majestic music of the invisible
the *ah!* waterfalls of sound there unceasingly sonorous gushing

Music of the unmanifest real world to which
the tinkles of laughter and sawing of groans in this world are only
echoes just as images of blood and guts and smiling
faces are only faint and fuzzy imaginings compared with the

actual high-pillar'd court and gorgeously rolling green hills and
cliffs of that world which is the true source of

this one we so blindly wander down
attracted by a sound a trumpet a sweet voice
looking for an open door

4/10

3   O SHARP WIND

O sharp wind
(turning corners ruffling hair)
you've traveled from so far to get here
whipped water into waves enhancing the
work of the deep machinery of churning currents
blown coats equally of diplomats and dipsomaniacs
sculpted the outlines of elephants and ants (who miraculously
hold to the ground till you pass)
your invisible gunshots blowing holes and flinging debris
loosening roofs and rattling windows
chasing hats and newspapers then suddenly
dropping them at the feet of strangers
whistling and warbling singing a single note with
multiple modulations both sound and no sound
yet almost decipherable words formed in
breathy enunciation messages from distant
planetary corners to the bristling cheeks and closing eyes of these
passersby attempting to walk through you
hearing but not heeding your words

4/12

4 OUT OF A DRIP A WHOLE WORLD

Out of a drip a whole world comes floating into view
like creatures in an aquarium the
glare of the glass blinding us gargantuan and
minute things crawl through the water
whole islands of life ringed by coral reefs and atolls
from a tiny drop no bigger than the tear that's
sliding from your eyes of
grief or gladness the emotional engine that
moves the world into existence from deep
darkness to this curiously visible
remnant of a Paradise too soon wavering to us its
fond memories of pale lagoons and purple
skies its delicacies of sight and sound these
bands of light and waves of distant
mockingbird arias remind us of
the utterance God made to us itself the
flora and fauna of our primordial state
His Words the green ferns whose fronds are the
vegetative lexicon we read to remind us of that
generous spray of drops on our foreheads each
drop of which is in itself a
world

4/13

5   THE SOUND OF IRON TRAIN WHEELS

The sound of iron train wheels against iron track
squeak and thrum

The famous clack though not as
regular as you'd think

till it gets up to speed
the air-conditioning sound of the

train itself
Septa to Trenton

The sometimes whispering wheels like a subway and
the rocking-back-and-forth-on-springs sound

passing blighted brick and streets going off to the sides
toward what adventures what human worlds

What human ruin and wrack?

4/16

6   IN A VERY CLEAR DREAM

In a very clear dream I was told about the
invention of a paper that cuts other paper
and suddenly I was demonstrating it for a
group of people

I had a roll of what seemed like waxed paper
I cut a piece that actually turned out to be a
wedge-like sliver and held it a bit
stiffly in my hand

pulled another sheet taut and sliced the
sliver clean through separating the
sheet from its anchored side all the while

talking it up like any
product salesman

4/18

7 IF WE FELT THE EARTH MOVE UNDER US

If we felt the earth move under us
in its flow
wherever it goes

If we sometimes almost had to hold on
as the globe turned
and could sense its revolutions its fleet
swiftness round its axis and even
forward through space as well
riding it
as we walked to the corner grocery or
crossed a street and could also
look up at the sky and see
signs of its graceful movement against perhaps the
slower clouds or backdrop of whatever
weather

Not hearing it move through space necessarily
no whistling or wind of its merry-go-round trajectory
but still could sense under our feet under these
solid bodies of pumping pulsations we've been
given to ride in for a time
the ride of the planet as well

If we felt this both poignantly and serenely
would it change us much in regards to
our peacefulness or maybe especially
our place in the universe

Would the feeling of the flow of roundness moving also
around under us change the forward
landscape of our lives or change our
way with each other or with

He Who is both absolute movement and
absolute stillness

If we felt the earth move under us
in its flow?

4/18

8 WHY IN NEW YORK

Why in New York does the loudest and heaviest
machinery get used in the absolute
middle of the night
way down on the street somewhere the
shouts of men and the whine and counter-whine of
hugest gears and screaming iron dump-scoops and
thump of tonnage as if the
ghost of the Titanic were trying to haunt so-called civilization in
retaliation for all its turbines and smoking funnels going
down
high-pitched squeal-beep backing-up squeal-beep
squeal-beep squeal-beep
washed over by the mechanical
surf-noise and crunch-growl of something like a
monster-flattener so that where ancient
myths leave off for which we are often so
poignantly nostalgic for the darker simpler days of yore
where the natural elements and their emissaries were
more directly part of our lives
Grendel grabbing us and eating us whole for example
Scylla and Charybdis squeezing the life out of us as we
try to pass straight through

These raucous machines carry on
New York in the middle of the night when maybe
no one but me may be trying to sleep
the gory giants of yore those yory giants gorily
go on

Listen to the iron shuttle-cock bang on the ground down
there

passing bus sneeze fire truck yowl
giants unsleepily roaming the city gnashing their machinery teeth
happily at home

4/19

9　THE LICKING SOUND

The licking sound of a thousand tongues licking
nectar off leaves

The sound of light falling slowly behind mist
nebulous Niagaras in veils of scintillant particles

The sound of distant animal sighing and the even further
sound of antlers clacking in a distant sun-drenched glade
dry ringing sound of bone against bone
melodious as water

The subtle rustling of leaves turning to catch rays of light
the forward rush of time as it flows
majestically through itself gathering
everything in its wake like rows of rowboats
tied to a wharf unable to keep from
bobbing when a liner booms through

The sound of a clear call coming closer past every other sound

The sound of the tiniest hair growing

The sound of eyesight getting dim
turning everything inward to where there is no sound
birds scrambling in a bush
elegance of every precious thing falling slowly or
rising to the surface as if in a flood

The cry turns out to be the world itself
presenting itself to Eternity

And Eternity nods to acknowledge it
and turns everything to pure light

with a soft ticking sound

4/21

The animal that most resembles me
is the animal I want to be

House-wrecker fat-faced weasel-eyed lion-hearted
wildebeest-stinkeroo slither-puss dragon-breath'd
pigeon-butt dog-faithful bird-brain mongoose of a
sack-o-snakes in delightful Technicolor to come
after you in one body cackling and crowing and
bellowing like a ghost with its
head in its hands
marching down the highway like a
sky full of geese
shy as a gold fish

That's the one I want to be

The animal that most resembles me

4/23

11 CONSCIOUSNESS

Consciousness is more like a chimney than a room
more like a flue a tube a conduit tunnel a
channel a glass funnel greater than the
Himalayas more like an
inverted pyramid of highly charged mist of
atoms making a vast vertical thoroughfare
than a palace of blond ice or plateaus each with a
particular pagoda on them or a globe unless it's a
globe of greater-than-the-earth-itself proportions

It's where we are and are not
in that we don't
interfere with the workings of the universe around and
within it
it's coterminous with all
but the essential

It's that beyond the sensual horizon of
natural structures consciousness looms or maybe is even just a
tenuous thread stronger than spider web
like a kind of transcendent fiber-optics between
the cosmic Unseen where all
really real things take place

And this puny person of ours who can
just stand in front of Victoria or Niagara
Falls for example with our

hands at our mouths in utter and
complete astonishment

4/26

12 IN CROSSING THE BUSY STREET

"There are 8 million stories in the naked city"

— THE NAKED CITY

In crossing the busy street the man
turned his head at the last moment to avoid
collision with a great rumbling truck with
squeaky springs and gasping pneumatic brakes and at the
last minute turned his head back again in the
direction to which he was going

and found himself on another street in another
city in another country altogether and shook
himself awake but wasn't asleep and
heard unknown words all around him from a
language he thought he'd never heard before and also thought
of all the stories where the protagonist spends
almost a full lifetime somewhere else after
dipping a bucket into a river then snaps
back to that spot still filling the bucket and sees that
actually only a few seconds have passed and the bucket's not even full

The idea flashed through his head and was gone before he
could really even think about it turning into a
side street that went all the way to the
glistening brown ribbon of a large busy river
where barges filled with cattle negotiated
creamy rapids frothy at the tips

A door at his right caught his attention
without hesitation he entered hoping to be in an
emerald-paneled palace with dragon fountains smoking
pungent incense in blue puffs out jeweled mouths in which he could
discern both his past and future to make up for the
perplexity of his present
but it was only a small webby shop selling tea

He took a cup from the smiling proprietor who didn't seem to
mind this total stranger in modern dress
who had none of the currency of the realm
whatever that realm might be out a
window coral mountains and a silvery
waterfall the flowing script of herons in flight
across a nearly turquoise sky

But I don't know if I can sustain this fantasy much longer
in a deli off Times Square called appropriately inappropriately

Belly Delly in the upstairs seating area with the radio blaring
and enough tables for about fifty or more
people but totally and eerily deserted at 10:30 P.M. overlooking
Caroline's Comedy Club on Broadway as lit up and gaudy as Las Vegas with
people in sociable clumps or striding long-legged and purposeful or
standing
hailing taxis or sliding by on bicycles
and the woman DJ has just read a
vaguely touching poem by Rod McKuen of all people

I wonder what happened to him
an old man now in really battered tennis shoes somewhere in San Francisco
or shoeless somewhere
dead

4/27

2

The mountain had never before experienced such elation
as soon as he set foot on it
it began to sing

Even the rocks had eyes for the clouds
and the clouds reciprocated by sending down dew

Circles of light flew in every direction
and his face was calm
one step forward seeming to cross ages
both of himself like the rings of a tree
and the world like a casual remark
that sends armies into the plain
to do battle with falsely imagined enemies

He turns his head as he climbs
a steep stairway cut into rock
toward a monastery in an improbable
place on a jutting cliff beyond what can be conceived of as

possible to build on hanging out into space

silence all round him and a soft

plucking sound

4/28

3

And now I'm back in my room above 5th Avenue
at 5 in the morning
and I've left the man whom we'll call L
somewhere in a distant land from where he
began and I just

woke from a dream I can't remember so he
might be stranded in the land of
unremembered dreams say or
a place between the beams of a sunset or a place that
takes place when a battle takes place that's simply
too much for people to bear such as
Kosovo or Bosnia and a dimension makes itself

available out of compassion for people who need to
get lost in far from the noise and stench of
death and the palpable odor of fear

so let's look at his face let's look into his
eyes to see if we can see what he sees
some clue to where he is and how he
might be returned to the cross-street he disappeared in

He's round-faced like the moon
deep-lidded eyes and almost perfect lips
nostrils well-defined ears symmetrically placed
an evenness and openness of forehead and gaze
and the eyes like two floating paper lanterns in
Venice or Kyoto
always in a state of sweet surprise
and through these eyes coming toward us
are the last miles he's climbed or clambered
onto a train in a state of exhaustion deciding
this world is not the world to anchor his
hopes in

The door's always open

It just depends on which side of the inside
you want to be on

4/28

4

There are so many places we've been that we'd like to revisit
drawing back to their actual physical sensations

touching them all over again brushing our
lips against them even a springtime day in a
foreign country

And it's there where L is now exactly where I
left him but in the space and time
not of the past as our memories purport to be
though some memories may be actually hiding out in the
future behind a broken lattice wall or yellow fog
though I'm trying now to remember with my
head in my hands my thumb pulling my beard-hairs my
eyes squeezing shut to make a
light behind them to see by
exactly where I envisioned him being last night when I was
simply too tired to continue this exploration

I think he was in the air but I can't be sure
and I'm not so sure I want him there
maybe better on a boat

Ah now I recall and also why he's so hard to
contact why there's such a silence around him where
he's concerned he made it up to the cliff and he's
sitting in the monastery there at the height of
soaring eagles and blinding white clouds

He's in a giant brown room with a handful of
adepts and an ancient master so old even the
dust doesn't bother landing on him anymore
he's more like paper than flesh and his
thoughts and words are more like texts than conversation

So L is there having a bowl of rice and inhaling the
incense and listening just as we're tuning in to him
past the noise of a distant door-bang and past the
bell a lone monk at the opposite end of the
monastery is ringing in his solitary cell

He's listing to the almost inaudible flap of eagle's wings
in the high space around him
and also somehow to the space the eagle's flying in
which he has grown so astute right now as to be
able somehow to "*hear*"
so it doesn't matter exactly what dimension he's
in in regards to us trying to reach him or me
trying to retrieve him for my own literary purposes

He's completely content to be where he is
and where he is is very remote from
human communicative concerns

There's a thin blue light trickling down inside him
with a yellow beam filtering down behind it
and an eagle of pure light flying slowly around them both
soft wing-flaps in the high air
and I've a good mind to leave him there

crossing the street
miles from everywhere

4/30

5

I've always had the feeling I've abandoned him somewhere
yet he pops up in the most amazing places
never quite sure which dimension to appear in
his face turned perpetually toward our original home
yet the bronze cast to his features the suggestion of a
smile through the various vicissitudes that visit him
he pops up in water standing to his waist cupping
generous splashes of it over his head smiling at the sun
he appears running alongside a train as it pulls out of a
station not really bidding farewell and perhaps even
not there at all just a blur in the air

He sits in a remote corner of a formal dining room in
Austria reading a book waiting for his meal
or perhaps he's writing one
and then when I look up again he's gone

He's the echo inside the echo inside the echo of a
childhood memory of the arrival out of nowhere of an
unknown uncle who's traveled the world
as you listen at your bedroom door long after you've been
sent off to bed
the deserts of China and Mongolia Brazilian rainforests African markets
and yet he's only in his
twenties

he looks out of the haunted eyes of the homeless
from his vanished kingdom

out of the burn victim's bandaged head staring from his death
out of the elephant's small heavy-lashed eyes as he
stands patiently swaying from side to side

and he wakes you up with a start as he
says your name in a way no-one's ever said it
before not with simple
familiarity but something more as if he's had

knowledge of its meaning and your meaning
forever

but when you turn to answer him
he's gone

5/2

6

He stepped off the curb and stepped onto it again
waiting for the traffic to pass

The inelegant circus with its ill-fitting clothes and
grinding gears

And straightens his jacket and pulls at his shirt
and feels his body inside his clothes and blinks

Looks to the right and
steps off the curb again

And crosses the street
and is gone

5/2

13 EVERY SOUND IN THE COSMOS

Every sound in the cosmos got trapped one day in a
giant glass cube of silence
on a hill of new ferns

As soon as the sound was inside
it started to glow and lit up the whole sky

Every bird-chirp harp-pluck bell-ring door-slam
pipe-stem-clench toboggan-swoosh airplane-drone
two-at-a-table outdoor terrace gossip tennis-serve lob-pop
ocean-roar surf-hiss gull-cry sky-boom

even the almost soundless expanse-sound of the sky itself
and the usually inaudible rumble of the earth as it creakily turns
and the faint sighing sound of the moon longing for its
origin somewhere in the Atlantic
and every heartbeat rat-a-tat of every
person on earth walking or sitting or sound asleep

each egg in its quiet hum
each sperm in its anxious and excitable wriggling high-pitched whistle

And silent clouds passed overhead
and silent light bathed the cube in supernal splendor
and for a moment people saw things as they really were

with a vision so complete
you could hear a pin drop

5/8

14 ALL THE LITTLE LEGS THAT CARRY US

All the little legs that carry us
tapping the earth as they strike out under us
propulsion robots set into motion by our
own particular whatevers
mind will desire life-force snap decisions to go
somewhere other than where we are so our
little legs carry us there
like hitting typewriter keys to spell out a
particularly knotty sentence only these words being
actions from A to B to C to D
incomprehensible except to the All-Comprehending

and at D some of us have little
wings we open
and fly away

5/10

15 A DESIRE TO READ OVID

I'm on the train to Trenton doing my crossword
when I've got a tremendous desire to read Ovid
but I don't have any Ovid
somehow my headspace wants mythic light-space
multiple transformations in a lurid blue sky
so I'll have to do it myself with the
passengers on board

The old man at the end of the seat who nearly wouldn't
let me in with his bright yellow baseball
cap and hearing aid
fell in love with a nymph in his well-spent youth
but before he could consummate his
love her more powerful suitor half-horse half-man
transformed him within a very short time
by the side of a lovely Grecian pool
into this codger clearing his throat reading the paper
the centaur of time having caught up with him as it
gallops alongside each of us with its
bow and arrow raised

Or this Latino mother and gorgeous round-faced
very Indian-looking little boy all excited looking out the

window in front of me as the train slides by the newly green
world of trees yards cars and gray backs of buildings
she's the queen of a heavenly realm he's a
prince of wisdom disguised as a child
the son of a lightning-filled cloud left over from the
Mayan dynasty
who crossed a river on a raft and the
boatman recognized her sovereignty
so he had to be turned into an eagle to fly protectively
over her head in the unseen realm even over our fast-moving train and
she was transported to this time and place with her
son and now looks less like a queen and more like a
normal woman speaking Spanish endearments from time to time to her
wide-eyed blue-blood genius pressing his tiny brown
nose against the glass

5/11

16 MEMORIAM

I

Last night at 6PM my mother was drawn
through the eye of a needle

Her shadow erased from its cloud above the lake
her sound of shallow breathing and eyeblinks
absorbed back into the silence that sits in the center of light
and generates white noise over valleys rooftops seas and copses
her exact position in time and space
at every moment vacated suddenly and absolutely
a tiny current of air rushing into the body-shaped
vacancy she left behind
having inhabited so very little at the end of her long life
and having inhabited a stern but modest amount in the
earlier portion never raising her voice very high even when
a little tipsy which was rare even through the 1920s
happy in laughter and absorbed in a wry geniality most of the time

The last napkin's dabbed the corners of her mouth
the last urinal emptied the last pills ingested

She opened her eyes wide a few moments before she

died delighting her caretaker who told her how grateful she was
and how much she loved her

I learned of her death on the other side of the country though no
presence is required at a Neptune Society cremation
so in a few days she'll fill a small envelope or shoe box or
piece of Tupperware with a snug-fitting lid and then be
drifted over the disinterested waves of the Pacific who'll
roll her along then deep into their long whale song
then into a resounding as deep as the sound of a gong

5/12

2

She wiped my face and bottom
took me downtown on a bus to see Bambi
drew Gibson Girls with always the same
pert profile and spit curls for me whenever I asked
though I have to go far back to childhood to
really remember her sweetest motherliness
that Buddha-like 1940s distance of parenthood in its own nimbus
unreachable idol in its own niche
while being in actuality another mortal just like ourselves

though forever inhabiting a royal paternal realm
going now in relation to me to where those personages always go
a special palace in the Unseen reserved for parents

My mother my last parent alive in this life
parent of my flesh my liver brain and heart
genetic parent of my teeth and eyes and cheeks
fingers toes and hair
and now her hair is gone her eyes unseeing with
one unseeing glance upward before she went
taking in every car ride we took every shopping trip
every birthday present opened every Thanksgiving
quick bow of the head before eating
every porch and wicker-chair moment in our yearly
rented-for-two-weeks Lake Tahoe summer cabin
every shared inside joke and occasional secret though I
can't at the moment remember any maybe there
weren't any maybe I only wished there
had been

maybe I only wished for a mother I never had
though the one I did have
now is gone

3

I wonder where she'll go
she wasn't sure she wouldn't commit she thought she'd
wait and see and now she'll know
the paisley curtain drawn aside as it were
the lengthy tunnel traversed perhaps
the earth so still so very eternally still
each growing thing now growing in silence
no earthly sound again every whisper
magnified every thought melodious or scored
scorched or torch-lit heavens redolent of stars
in which to see her source
the long of it now become the short
the wait-and-see now become at last
darkness visible the
long call home
the very vivid recognition of the soul

4

Sparkling lagoons for you my sweetheart mom
who's become more my ancient daughter than my mom

How you became confused and infantile at the
end of a life more or less of leisure

So boats down slow canals lying back on pillows for you
mother
reunited with dad in a place you both would like

something with water
reflections (but not too much self-reflection) more like
glittering light and shadow against your faces
as you float along

Sitting on beach chairs for you and cool drinks
certainly Paradise
you were both always generous and giving
and if I wanted something more from you than you could give
that was me not you after all

So glittering mountaintop lakes for you
and a large barge on a dark river

And all the sweetmeats you can eat
in a day of perpetual sunlight

5/13

17 THE HUSH SOUND

The hush sound of something happening across a river
of a crackle in the air overhead an electric
snap in nothingness
of two live wires touching and the
sound of falling sparks
each falling into its own silence its own
darkness like tiny ignited demon elevators going down their
own shafts into their own hells

A sound above the upper registers in a
language that is mostly a motion like ice over
snow followed by snow and black sky

The sound of a small mammal struggling as it dies
and currents moving through opposing currents deep
undersea

above which
high above which

enormous golden air stretched everywhere

5/15

18 SMALL ALABASTER PIPETTES

Small alabaster pipettes that emit a tiny
wind sound when blown across their tops
an upper register note particularly apprehended by
dogs when the air stream is more purposefully blown
these were first found in China at the court in the
Forbidden City not part of the
official survey and almost lost forever when mislabeled as
drinking straws
though being so far from the others maintained that
error
until food-focus lost its ubiquity as answer to every
question and motive for every archeological find
so there's the courtly high-pitched whistle from these
delicately carved pipettes
and a small shell-shaped jade item with a similar flute embouchure
opening that also makes a surprisingly deeper
wind sound and that looks like something you'd
find among washed-up debris on the beach
and which even seems to have stored up wild
sounds of sea surf and sky in its tiny molecular sonorities
and then there's an ivory-like box made of some truly
unknown unknowable substance
heavy as lead and seemingly solid but not in

fact though you'd be hard put to see how it's
not when it seems like a paperweight heavy through and through
yet when you lift and tip it even slightly
it makes an eerily beautiful chime-sound but as if from
far away and like distant
tinkly melody
wind-chimes or door-chimes and with numerous
overtones and semi-quavers unusual in any
tone row but exceedingly pleasing to the ear especially when
coupled with the shell and pipette notes to create an
actually full though delicate orchestra of sounds extremely rarified and
uncanny in nature very much like this
poem itself describing them since they really don't even
exist except for a time in this
tuned mesh of words
in which they are almost visible
almost viscerally sensible and smelling of sea-wrack
and almost audible since I've gone to so much trouble

describing what is actually only a
non-existent wraith created out of whole cloth

You can hear their ghostly ensemble now
if you lean forward just a little bit

and imagine as clearly as you can a small herd of horses
so black they're purple

running along a beach at dawn
against a blinding white sea

5/17

New York City's not built for repose
it's built for razzle-dazzle
it's built to be brilliant in
the skyline hasn't usurped nature
it acts as if nature never existed
it says here's an anthology of interesting buildings
of geometric shapes in all sizes and angles to show off their
best sides like glamour shots of very serious movie stars
finicky about lighting
facades and rooftops and over at least a billion lit windows

I'm alone out on the balcony of the 5th Avenue
sixteenth floor penthouse apartment of
friends spooning leftover tofu soup into my mouth looking at the
Empire State Building at night with its red white and blue
lights beaming upward along its facades like
lights on a juke box with bright blue up the
spire pointing into a rosy gray sky
the hum of mechanical energy all around me

and I drown in this sea

20 GOD'S NEEDLE

O God You thread us through the eye of a needle
with such ease

Then with the thread we sew a life as
You see fit

Some long and luminous
some done with a couple of passes through the cloth

Some tuxedos in a blur of lights
some scarecrows with straw out the sleeves

Some robes of honor around bodies of luminescence
in which Your essence is the form and meaning

Each gesture from Your plan always in motion
in sky or ocean across lofty turbulence or choppy seas

We reach the extent of the pattern You have cut for us
neck-holes for head arm-holes for arms

in blazing asbestos cloth that goes unscathed
or ignited like a torch in Your fierce gaze

Wrapped tightly or unwrapped and seeming to float
each of our lives unique in time and space

Until our allotted thread runs out
and we're folded in our pilgrimage cloth

having reached its term
then tucked under sheets in earth's hard bed until Your

horn is blown

5/20

21 SUDDENLY THE GREAT QUESTIONS

Suddenly the great questions were about to be
answered once and for all

how the universe began the exact size and
shape of space what really happens after
death who is this deity we're
meant to rely on

The shadow of the answers was coming down the
stairs the blinding marble stairs cut from
the answer-world to this world of unending
questions thrashing like a sea

Why are we separate and alone

Where is unity among antagonisms

Why is death necessary

What is the soul

And first everything became dark as pitch
and a wind of vastness began blowing uncontrollably

freeing the molecules in our bodies to take
rearranged shapes from silent oyster at the bottom of the sea
holding a giant pearl translucent with promise
through all the creeping crawling and standing
creatures to actual starlight
radiant through space-corridors their
slant-beams traveling endlessly
and the shadow of the answers was coming down the
stairs

And the darkness lifted suddenly
and a leaf shone out of the air with tiny writing on it

and a grotto appeared out of nowhere with water dripping
and each drop inscribed with the
same tiny script as the leaf

and the air glittered all around illuminating
the intricate text of leaf and drip
drop of lark tip of dart and dark part of the deepest heart

as day passed and dunes were shorn of light

earths moved from edge to edge
and a lone voice whispered in the night

5/23

22 OF THE DOLPHIN'S TONGUE

Of the dolphin's tongue and the rower's oar

and the arc of the iris as it arches over

of the giant motions of tiny shells

and dunes that turn as the whole sky swells

the thud of a rudder hitting shore

the thud of a shore as it oozes

articulation radical articulation iridescence

tiny bug on a tiny leaf stops to inspect a tiny speck

laughter in a lounge leaks out into the street

laughter in a lopomobile as it lunges

23 IS IT ALL JUST A SEA OF WHITE CLOUD

Is it all just a sea of white cloud after all
all our sighing and longing

a sea of cloud from one end to the other
with evenly dimpled dips and blemishes

and at the slight arc of the earth's curvature
a sizzle of light rising into pure blue sky

of all our sighing and longing and heartache
after the great moments with their

elaborate processions and clatter of leggings and occasional horses
the shouts of opprobrium and their echoes that for all we know

fill the entire universe including its
small birds new buds and any hidden

hollows in space that might actually be the
opposite side of its fullness rather than any

notion of emptiness which could
account for these feelings when the last foot and final cry have

left the arena of our dazzled consciousness and moved
on to a neighboring universe perhaps to

celebrate another
leaving us as if in an empty banquet hall

with God's breath still on the glass rims
and the movement of chandelier crystals delicately

back and forth in the equally delicate
movement of the air and the sound of the

soft tinkling of previous blessings filling our
ears

5/31

24 THE LIGHTS HAVE BEEN LIT

The lights have been lit for a major event
tiny electric filaments ignited by lightning-like
juice enough to burn incandescent
orange where before there'd have been a
chandelier lowered and candles lit for the
night room to be in daylight enough for us to see our
hands in front of our faces and the faces of
loved ones floating out of the dark their
incandescent eyes both
shining and seeing eyes of
telescopes for the soul eyes of horizons unto
themselves the very eyes that rest on top of the
heart like lakes on top of volcanic rifts
so alive with their own light and into whose
widths only a face wide whole
worlds flood in whole hillsides in sunlight whole
circus tents full of elephants on parade holding
flags in their trunks whole
oceans of waves like giants thrashing in their sleep having
dreams of sight even
imagining everything we're going through as if it were only an
endless blank wall of mist projecting it onto us
and at the end of it a tiny room just big enough to hold

the form of light we long to clasp to our
inner form whose music is almost too pure for our
poor souls to bear
we have to hear clanking and loud drunken
piano-clunks in between us and
the beloved's form which is really no
form at all
appearing out of eternity's wall

6/4

25 A HUMBLE BEEHIVE

It's a humble beehive that stands halfway
between the North 40 and the highway

a normal hive-shaped hive on a platform
and because our great grandfather'd just come over from
Rumania and was dirt poor
he only had one
but when you get up to it it sounds like a
thousand

You've never heard such a commotion such an
orchestra of buzzing you'd expect the hive to be
levitating off its base right into the
sky the buzzing's so intense and even
more than intense it's
multi-layered it's got bass buzzes and very high almost
inaudible buzzes and when it's quiet all around
the hive seems to actually be
speaking
English
words and sentences and whole
speeches like normal folks I was

out there one dusk when everything becomes
hushed and listening to the hive and I heard
the sonorous buzzing of the bees say

Live along the line of light you've been given
Go nowhere that's not hallowed ground

In the east where the sun rises is the
preparation for sunset

The Lord walks through here with honeyed
feet on His way to the
threshing of souls

We are His serenaders we are the
doctors of mankind

6/5

26 EVERYTHING BECOMES A CARPETWORK

Everything becomes a carpetwork for other feet to tread
in the cyclotorium of our being
that is such a labor of love that we construct
phrase by phrase lifting the roof beams
for air to take place in enough for song to float

Unbeknownst to ourselves it's
all for others to enjoy in the midst of their
labors

As we have also tread on another's design
that is more a palatial room than a
carpet although it is a place to stand
for their own construction to be built on
and the design of flying birds from thickets
intricate in their brambly weave and
open glades utterly sun-drenched water
running to the four corners from a
central source

Nothing is left to chance
though a feather float down at its own soft pace
and land at our feet from another

country altogether from an unknown
sky denizen its outline of blue sparks its
shaft of electricity feathery at the edges

Love is the mesh the weave and the thread
the weaver is love

The pattern that emerges is
love's lights

Mercy is the key

6/8

If you're waiting for another moment than this one to be the
Supreme Moment know
there is only this moment
and no other

If you're waiting to look out a train window in the
Andes at languid blue fog puffs
rising from imponderably deep gorges
or to breakfast on a tiled terrace in Venice or
Tunisia with glorious golden bougainvillea waterfalling down

it won't happen exactly as you so fervently hope
it won't happen with harp music or bright light from eternity flashing
any more than the peculiar harp music of this train-squeak and
people-murmur and the leaking light of eternity that
already flows from your face

If you hope against hope that a door will open
and an image of God appear in its radiantly lit rectangle
cloudy arms outstretched in greeting and a
strong scent of jasmine
this door will have to do this very window this very space
and the image of God you search for is certainly
the light of what you're seeing right now

If you want time to stop altogether in one fine
heartbeat or one with your right foot
raised before stamping or the split second before one
thought chases another into oblivion

the green deer in this forest have already vacated their
shadows and emerald
outlines in nothingness mark where their
warm bodies had been

all the ferns trembling where God's feet so recently passed

the air bright with His smile

6/9

28 LIKE LILACS

Like lilacs like ladders on fire
leading down

Like watching the passage of time out a small window

Like purple that bursts into red at the black end

Like black when it wants to surround us and
drown us

We think one thing one moment about death and its
deserts its long marches its hurts its bedbugs
but it's lateral it's a spaceship out of here it's
never-never land it's bittersweet sweet-bitter

its sandpaper smoothes down the rough edges

Death is an *I-don't-know* that's beyond being humble

It's a loud knock on a locked door
we've never heard before

It's the way out and the way in
not drawn on the floor

Death's a radiolarian in a class experiment we
leave behind all summer so when we go back in the Fall
we don't know what to expect

Death's eternally unexpected
cosmically inspected by Number One
it's a place in the sun

I don't know what to say about death so
I'll say anything

The striped rooster in the loud hen yard
headlessly announces the dawn

The whole town wakes up
to find it's gone

My mother died
but she's alive inside

6/11

29 JESUS SAT ON A ROCK

Jesus sat on a rock amid the flames
and slowly and eloquently pronounced each name
of insect flower ditch cloud gate and harness
in order to release us from Adam's original
blessing which had become a curse
overlooking a thunderous ocean whose pounding waves
were also eloquent and whose watery syllables
also named both the great and small leaving absolutely
nothing out no nuance of psychic perturbation
moon-phase cloud-shape color of day or night and constellation

Finally Jesus arose and every water level on
earth rose with him every creature's body lifted slightly
and each being was re-infused with divine ringing
as in a cluster of harmonious chimes
running through their scales a million times in almost inaudible
tones so that we see that now every atom and every
atom's nucleus vibrates
from being called upon again by
Sublime Clarification's voice
setting it apart from mere chaotic noise

6/12

30 SAY THE EMERALD'S GREEN

Say the emerald's green and lies in the heart of the forest
the panther's black and slinks to his destination
the rain is a curtain of crystals pulled at a slant
the toads are miniature Volkswagens sitting on lilypads
a quadrilateral heart of light turns rapidly above the lake
the whole thing's a dream told by someone half-awake
under a dome of convex glass

Say this reality or that reality the giraffe still eats
topmost leaves the blind mole plows through dirt
what flies lands on the tip of your finger and zooms away
God's perfection reflected in the world His constant reflection
though He's unlike anything in it of it from it or above it

The prince in his chamber dressing in ermines
the pauper as consciously fastidious in rags
the old horse weary submitting to glue-hood
dreaming to itself its meadowy youth

Say it all resolves itself in the snap of a finger
this room with its piles of books and papers
dawn birds in trees outside singing like crazy
another day to realize the perfect anemone

6/13

31 ACHIEVE

I may not be able to achieve what I've
hoped to achieve

so perhaps I should stay just inside the
shadow of the cave-mouth

instead of sitting outside in the sun

6/14

32 TOPKNOT OF ROSES

The topknot of roses that emerges just as
emerging from the dream-cave to
waking takes place slowly but startlingly

and then we're here in recognized simplicity
and the stables where all my friends were
standing like horses are no longer forever

but here is also not forever and no longer or
not much longer than a lifetime in dimensional length
and we'll wake up from this one with its perhaps more

high definition details of who's doing what
which girlfriend who becomes a wife which
nephew who becomes a criminal which acquaintance who

becomes a famous Shakespearean actor
we wake up one day from this one and everything's become
classically still as if pillars of alabaster

stairways of marble echoes of ancestors
echoes of ourselves coalescing and drifting apart
echoes of realities fully emerge from our hearts

and stand before us

6/19

33 MY FATHER'S HANDWRITING

I've got some samples of my father's handwriting
found in a drawer when my mother died
and it's curiously unique and poignant to me
the way he made letters the very tall ascenders like
sentinels with backwards flags on top
a certain roundness of the writing almost
medieval half-script half-printing a real very
private artistic flair though he had no
pretensions it was
just the way he wrote
the way snow sticks to the tops of mountains
long after winter's gone further down

They're paper-clipped together sheets from his old
office pads with the trucking company
logo I remember from 1940s childhood
printed in blue in a circle in the middle
at the top of each sheet
notes to cousins in Texas asking
questions of family genealogy
the handwriting so different from mine so
conscious of itself it seems
blackberry brambles by the side of public roads
surprisingly sweet berries in their
scratchily barbed tangles

These flowing letters formed by my father's right hand a
few years before he died carrying with them for me
the remembrance of him making them his
concentration in a pool of lamplight
mythic beast at the mouth of a cave half-
snoozing half-vigilant both silent aggressor and
defender of his domain
by the carefully wrought letters flowing out from
under his hand
a somber music sounding long
after his death
in a little box now by my Philadelphia bed

6/21

34 I WAKE UP

I wake up on the far side of the moon
with silver tides billowing between the earth and me
and a night sky with Mars red as a welt
above disappearing heads of geese in flight

I left my beloved momentarily watching for any
trace of light
on an earth of violent street corners and
chopping waves

I'm going out now to find my beloved again
among the black and white canisters
keeping the constant source of love flowing out
from my deepest center across the heads of those

who've lost their heads completely and utterly
for love's investments

6/23

35 LAST PHRASE ADDRESSED TO ME BEFORE WAKING FROM A DREAM

What you call God
I call Mind

6/23

36 THIS ROSE

This rose has as many petals as windows in a major city
and since I'm in New York let it be New York

and at each window is a solitary person gazing out or just
standing still with no definite characteristic of either

looking out or in
faces placid eyes clear cheeks a little flushed hands at sides

gazing on either the passing outer circus or inside at the green
herbarium of both memories and their blissful eradication

into the cool steam of God's breath that flows across absolutely
everything as it grows from roots or crawls on legs or sails

cunningly between alternating leaves of shadow and light
and in each heart of each person at the window

is a rose
with as many petals as windows in a major city

and at each window stands an ancestor to the people at the
first windows and they are not so different from

the people of the first windows except for the
profusion of feathers and antler headdresses and the

ribbon shirts and long planetarily embroidered
sleeves of their garments

and within each of their hearts are also
roses with petals greater in size than the

known heavens and cosmological spheres
and at their stems the secret of the origin of all the

worlds quietly presses out its majestic and ferocious thorns
and within the open mouths of each rose a sound more

vast and deafening than the harshest cataract and cruelest
hurricane whose roar has been compared by its

victims to the onrush of a freight train at full throttle
and it is the song of the universe singing to itself and

bathing in the radiance of its echoes
and this is the voice of the Creator to the creation enunciating

each definite thing in specific and laciest detail
and it whispers in the stem in the heart of the

rose of the ancestors whose faces gaze out through the
petals of the roses in everyone's hearts who look

longingly or peacefully out these windows
which are the velvety and deep red petals

of this rose

6/24

37 SEVERAL RAINBOWS

Several rainbows gathered around a drinking straw
knowing they had an angelic mission but
getting momentarily confused so they
fluttered and irridesced nevertheless and the
drinker at that straw saw intense white
light and fell back in ecstasy

Then the red end of the spectrum suddenly remembered so they
detached themselves from the straw and
flew across town in an incandescent pinpoint
until they came to a poor blind farmer's
son who was just learning the harmonica

6/26

38 THE TALL MAN WHO WENT FOR A SHORT WALK

The tall man who went for a short walk
and came back a rooster
for example said the millipede marking time a thousand times
like a rippling fringe standing still

Or the girl who threw her lover kisses from a train
thinking he was getting smaller due to distance
when he was actually shrinking
and when they met again she was shocked to find
he was now only an inch tall

Or the sound of a dog growling that grew to the growl of a
waterfall
then went back to being a murmur though only a
moment before it had filled the room with its
canine conflagration

Yet everything stays more or less the same
once fashioned
until it's time to abandon form to enter the
utterly formless realm
where a smile is a sun surrounded by orbiting planets
and a flashing eye is a constellation sending its
light through the heavens

and to move from place to place is an
eon of so-called evolution each flutter of change
registered as a major evolvement
birds in the trees except that they suddenly
swell to the size of a symphony orchestra
then back to a few random tweets from
branch to branch
a few cheery hellos

as the millipede might say
before hurrying off on all its thousand legs
to wherever it is millipedes are always in such a flutter
to go

7/8

39 LAUGHTER IN THE NIGHT

Laughter in the night becomes lilting birdsong at dawn

A talk show on the radio in the bedroom becomes a
heart-to-heart live conversation by noon

The weak yellow nightlight left on in the hall becomes
a honey-golden sunny carpet strip with bare children's feet
running back and forth on it

The rough mythical beast snoring with its head on its
claws becomes a frisky Pekinese yipping by the screen door at flies

The night with all its haunted restless denizens of graves
becomes a busy intersection crowded with busloads of nuns

(Will this poem with its comparative hesitations
become at least a gushing river on its way to the open sea?)

Nothing stays the same in this transformative universe where
orbits of distant galaxies become the shimmering puddle on a
saucer with glittering chandelier crystals
reflected in concentric circles in it

The dust from the first particles become headcheese on the
newborn just now emerged slippery as a fish from the womb
the light in its eye the very light of the final apocalypse
the gurgle of joy in its throat the same as the strange
watercourse cascading on Mars under its
dry visible crust seemingly a dead wasteland forgotten

The nuns in their bus busy with their subvocal rosaries
the same as the very quiet undersea maneuvers of
Paleolithic octopuses hiding under rocks

The sunlight on your face the same as the
saintly illumination once in a lifetime that turns the
saint's life entirely around as the fig tree he or she
sits under quietly bursts into bloom

7/12

40 WE SPILL OUT OURSELVES

We spill out ourselves
to the extent of ourselves
and push and pressure ourselves
beyond ourselves
turning like eager astronomers
to find more of the visible heavens
inside the hidden folds of ourselves
the biggest screen with the biggest projection
deep inside ourselves where
even all our own self's limits finally
melt away of themselves

7/13

41 IN A PINPOINT OF LIGHT

In a pinpoint of light on the edge of a surface
you'd expect to see eternity

In the loops of a gnat in front of your face at dusk
you might glimpse mortality

In the number of moods and faces of your beloved
you'd begin to suspect infinity has no end

In the sound of wheels grinding against iron tracks or asphalt road
the audible swift passage of time in its endless continuum of
traction against something always about to take to the
skies but remaining earthbound and getting older and a little
slower with each revolution becomes poignantly obvious
surrounded as we are by these glass domes of instruction
down whose endless corridors we pass hoping to
not have to quite come this way again to thread through the
same aisles and gaze at the same displays of
inflammable airplanes made meticulously out of toothpicks or
brown shrunken heads from Borneo with their lips and eyelids
sewn together with twine

but instead follow the glass domes into sunny meadows
where not only do we get the instructional displays inside
but reflections of bright baby blue sky and fluffy
clouds sliding along their round outer surfaces by day
and a dazzling planetarium display of stars and moon and
reddish pinpoint of Mars and bluish pinpoint of Venus by night

but also the flash of occasional otherworldly
oceanic wave-upon-overwhelming-wave of soul's illumination
by day or by night whenever the Divine Illuminator wishes us to know
that which lifts us bodily off our feet out of the
constant immemorial data of our lives

leading us to carry a bucket of clear water to the lone
fig tree on the hill overlooking the
tumultuous cascade and the bottomless chasm of echoes

where past and future twist in the air for a
moment like ribbons of birdsong tied in little knots
before disintegrating back into the air

7/14

42 A SHAKESPEAREAN DIALOG

Never could the incipient worm who
eats through us whole when we're sunk in the earth
until our forms are foam except for bones
pass himself off as the victorious one above-ground
by wearing say good Saks Fifth Avenue suits the
drape would be all wrong

or stand in our place at the head of a corporate conference table
as representing the real and ultimate us or
court our sweethearts with a wild blazer on
trying to smile a suggestive smile on those wormy lips of theirs
while they can barely stand up or pull themselves out
straight except as it propels them forward until they must

hunch up somewhere along their length to move at all
even though when the dust of our lives has settled and we're also
heroically trying to return to dust
and be unnoticed as humbly anything else but dust

worms are the final applause that follows our worldly performances
the final motherly compliments on our sharp looks or
slimmer bodies the Mother-Earth voice to soothe our
cares it's the worms singly or in chorus
who happily feast on our successes or failures once we're no

longer able to acknowledge them or even consciously play their
hosts except silently and all-too willingly
as they continue to animate our bodies and make good
use of us after we're dead unless we've reached an
incorruptible state in God's own preservational vault for true
martyrdom say on some wormless battlefield or in a

ray of godly light so strong no worm dare enter it even
after our death

7/16

43 A THOUSAND TINY BIRDS

A thousand tiny birds no bigger than thumbnails
flew out of a single egg

A single sentence regarding the beginning and end of all
life and philosophy emerged from everyone's lips at the
same moment as their ship dipped into the giant white
water-trough of a storm
and all their eyes straining together on the same spot
on the blackened horizon
became one wide-open eye with no
bloodshot veins around its silver-blue cornea

as a thousand tourists sipped a thousand perfect
café lattes in the Alps a wonderful pheasant the
color of pewter rainbows flew across the open expanse and
everyone felt a chill breeze on their cheeks simultaneously
thought about death and how they would
put their lives in order from that time onward

A single shot rang out and a thousand
birds now bigger than your open hand
turned abruptly in midair and flew south
into a cloud

A thousand clouds blew into the sky over a village
each one shading a particular house from the
blazing sun of an unusually blistering summer day
and a thousand children in identical T-shirts
came out of their doors and cheered
each T-shirt embroidered with the Chinese dragon of creativity
each face turned upward with flushed cheeks and looks of
wild and absolute expectation as the single hand of beneficence
passed slowly over their heads and withdrew again
into the thousand clouds

as a thousand birds now bigger than houses
landed on branches in the unseen and sang songs
the like of which no mortal has ever heard
nor will hear until our ears are exchanged for
ears of pearl and shell washed up on silent beaches
no water touches with its moist fingertips
nor smoothes with the flats of its soothing palms

7/17

44 WE LIVE IN THESE SMALL HOUSES

We live in these small houses the sizes of
slender gazelles
and spy in the distance mirrored steps
leading up to an incandescent cloud
and rivers bluer than ice flow out from its base
in circular formation until their waters actually
surround our shins and they're not
cold but oddly thick and soothing

The steps go up into what clears away to show a
mansion of wondrous proportions as they say
in that twenty Parthenons could easily fit into its
perimeters and acres of hilly very bright green slopes fall
away around it into dark forested grottos where
deeply melodious birdsong can be heard singing
"Come to us come to us"

And we see this and hear this and long for it from our
small habitations and we make
tentative moves toward it in our
frail gazelle's bodies with their
huge dark eyes and especially sensitive ears and a
heart that is somehow always virginal but
also somehow
so susceptible to the vagaries of mortal weather

7/22

45 TIME

A considerable amount of time is taken in its
intersection with space for which we have
God to thank for if not
flat and motionless we would be with our
noseless faces facing the sea for an
unmoving eternity in which schools of
shark for example would hang forever suspended their prey
at least always out of reach and those
desperate sharks losing both weight and
patience in pursuing in fact
nothing at all because they hang there flat and
menacing as blank sheets of very white
paper in the motionless water if there were no
space for time to move in

Love letters would never get sent and their
recipients like abandoned seals on an iceberg would never know their
amorous pursuer's intentions wouldn't feel their
heartbeats missing a beat or two out of
love for in fact even hearts could
skip no beats for without space to beat in hearts could
hardly beat but just sit like
monkeys on a fence gazing forever

stupidly at the air in which no utterly
ravishing beloved could move but only be a
stationary idea a psychological urge an idiotic
ideal always out of reach which would at least
subvert the settling into possibly tedious domesticity

String would not unwind yarn unravel ants
build spiders weave blobs of paint
travel across an expanse to become impressionistic
water lilies in a stretch of awesome gorgeousness

Were time to be absent from space or space from
time our inbreaths and outbreaths happy as
goldfish swimming peacefully round and round their
bowl with frail fins ribboning and
bubbles traveling from round goldfish lips to
break in the air of the surface at last
in which everything is perfectly circling in its
endless cycles and bicycles finally off into great God's even
greater cycles
would never occur

7/26

46 SIMPLY PUT

Simply put there is nothing that does not
glorify His Name

as I look out the train window at telephone
wires and trees

even bits of debris caught in track-side branches
having exhausted their usefulness such as a

tin can carton crate or truck tire tossed now
aside as we might be at any moment

as the great train glides by until to me
all's a colorful blur under a cloudy blue sky

intricate physicality dissolving behind me
there goes a tree a house a person in straw hat yellow pants

loping loosely by the side of the track
a red pickup truck a municipal building

as if absorbed into the wide mouth of some oceanic
neutralizer who flows ultimately across everything

each thing having called out God's Name with perfect
living strength repeatedly

as their wheels both big and small
as their hearts both brief and eternal

keep usefully turning

7/28

47 YOU'D THINK

for Asiya Levin

You'd think it would be such a simple matter
like calling a room to attention by striking a
glass with a spoon
to arrive at perfection with a whole new
sunrise coming out of your mouth and your head a
locus for angels with attendant light-shafts

Maybe utter generosity to all and whomever unceasingly
would pave the way with golden bricks

Maybe always being cheerful even with yourself in the
deepest solitude of your four walls with barred windows
while the seasons burst into bloom with
flags and canons and an endless stream of
edible cakes

Maybe a humility so profound even vermin
recognize it as being more humble and
disposable than they are

No shadow too long cast across your form down
any street in any gathering with everyone without
exception ignoring you as if you'd just told an
unfunny joke at a party that was just getting up steam

Clouds seem to gather without a problem
water falls gracefully so long as there's a
lower elevation to fall down

You'd think it would be such a simple matter
to let the happy dogs of the heart go free to
bound across one green valley after another to the
edge of the sea

and then for them to stand tails wagging on the
shore or dare to wade into it in the blazing
sun and their outlines as they go closer to the
water become really fuzzy until they
vanish into thin air and an even thinner sea
simultaneously

8/4

48 SAM THE SON OF SHEM

Sam the son of Shem
sat on a rock and pondered a fern

was the real world in the stem or the fronds
or in the space in between?

a thud
a rock the size of a head
clunked like a clod on the hard sod

a swish
of the smallish body of a fish in its
splash in the near marsh at dusk

sisters and brothers to rocks and twigs
consider it well
a few molecules to the right or left
and we'd be dust to tread on sea water in its
ceaseless see-saw teetering between tidal tug
flat and swell

Sam sat on the rock as
mosquitoes convoked converged and

conspired against him
though all he saw was angels hovering in a
cloud

a wisp in the air

a wisp of air suspended in air

with a little light flickering in its hair

kept him there

8/8

49 THE MAGIC DIVINE SPATTERINGS OF MESSAGE

The magic divine spatterings of message
stutter forward vertically

I woke up two days ago and my right foot felt like it had been
sprained in the night or whacked by something or
hacked at at any rate it hurt mightily and it was
in the muscle or tendon on the left side of the instep so I
hobbled around for a couple of days
"gout" someone said and my imagination filled with
18th century overweight English Ben Jonsons eating
pig fat drinking beer-swill none of which thank God
I do

But it's the first time I've really felt getting
old or vulnerable at least to bodily infirmity
bodily breakdown and its
ultimate unreliability
for two days acutely painful saintly foot
foot one of two but no less important for that
foot without whom I'm nearly useless
without which I'd be suddenly confined to something
inert and be really inert myself
saintly foot with wings on each side

Mercury's foot so fleet and purposeful when healthy
I owe you thanks for getting me here to
sixty-one and grateful seeing now how
without you I'd be

Foot so happily a part of me up ramps and ladders
running for trains or airplanes
dancing for joy as well as
leading me literally to temptation
never of your own accord it's true
as well as to illuminated circles of
remembrance
foot of bones and flesh and blood and muscle
touching the earth and holding my body upright as I go
God created and God blessed
like a building block which if taken away the whole
building falls down

The magic divine spatterings of message
stutter forward vertically

8/15

50 IT'S ONE OF THOSE EARLY AUGUST NIGHTS

It's one of those early August nights out on the
front porch on white wicker furniture with
cicadas in the trees creaking across either to each other or infinitely
out into the black cosmos to the stars

And a night-bird squeaks and crickets are in perfect
cricket rhythm multiple time-signatures plus
attendant earthbound car-tire noises as well as a distant
sky-bound airplane passing in the dark overhead

And all the sounds go out of sync for a
moment long enough for an imagined jungle beauty to come
as if parting huge leaves into a moonlight of openness
irradiating something more than human wisdom though perhaps

less than ultimate perfection
with almond-shaped incredible black eyes
darting slender incendiary glances
and a physical form somewhere between

water and the reverberations of an echo down endless canyons
but a certain bland though textured constancy takes over
as usual in God's pure creation
no creature green or otherwise materially appears

although against the gorgeous curtain of all this summer sound
the shadow of an imagined creature was
momentarily cast
and the actual atoms of its passing still

vibrate lightly to its tune

8/16

51   IF I SHOULD DIE IN THE NIGHT

If I should die in the night Lord
thread me back through the body-shaped hole that has
gotten me here to the source of its joy
from this physical form backwards O Lord
through geometrical garden plots and fractal dawns
throwing up their images as if they were real

52 IF I WANTED TO WRITE A POEM OF PURE JOY

If I wanted to write a poem of pure joy for everyone
how would I go about it
unless all the windows of my heart banged open either in
zoological unison or in a kind of botanical
succession in the sense that a
green stem might shoot up from deep subterranean
roots and push out velvety spade-shaped
leaves and then a torch-orange bud explode
fiery blossoms under a blue sky so utterly sun-drenched its
blueness puts all the delft blue of Holland to shame in its
utterly shameless blueness

Then music of course harps and lutes in full
concert plus a couple of Mariachi trumpeters
smiling like crazy potbellied with huge hats and black boots
and masses of children clanging clamorous bells

Then things floating in the air not just
banners or colored confetti but actual
words in full flight although slow enough to read such as
"anything from now on could be the spur to your complete enlightenment"
or *"swans glide across black lake water as elegant as clouds"*
or even just

*"the heartbeat you just had opened a door you're not even
aware of
up a stairway of light you're gliding along to a level you've never even
dreamed of"*
for example in order to
induce that sweet ecstasy of invitation just as you
are to a most importantly
satisfactory completion

*I swear a fly just landed on my
hand while writing this and stayed
on it as I walked across the room to the
screen door to let it out a most
unusual in fact uncannily peculiar occurrence in which it seems the*

*fly came to me specifically to be let out of the
room into the night from whence it
came its little green body and grid-prism'd multiple eyes on me
until I flicked it out in the air*

which is as simple a gesture of expansion as one could
get I suppose in this life as
all lives have life and the fly is one of God's most
ingenious if not most gourmet of creations

and so its joy at release and its relief not to have to
bat around inside a lampshade all night must be
experienced at some level of its "flyness"
it started by crawling up my leg onto my
finger

and ends by

celebrations in the moonlight that include
sleeping gray doves and English wrens with their
heads tucked under their wings

and will end with our waking up eyes wide mouths
agape in jubilation and wonder

as lights light up the horizon like a caravan of
fireflies on their way to an incandescence so bright even the
dawn has to take lessons from its splendor

and only the eyes of perfect saints are able to
patiently withstand it in the
silence of their perfect thunder

8/18

TO PAINT A PICTURE OR MAKE A SOUND

I

To paint a picture or make a sound in the
night like an opening of fiery peacock feathers in a
blaze of subterranean lights
across earth's bubbly curvature across which
very tall angels proceed with care but without
caution being of the angelic breed and so unaccustomed to
matter and its variously sticky involvements

To move forward in darkness to call out to cock an
ear in order to listen for a reply
to hear no reply but to continue nevertheless forward on all
fours if necessary hands and knees and even
forehead which upon contact with the earth becomes a
blaze of glory a palladium of lights and sheer
loftiness although descending deep into earth's
entrails in search of true humility

To sing out even a part of a word even only a
prefix to the long serenade of mortality fixed as if
a sacrifice of living flesh on the swiftly moving
antlers of migrating herds

a last gasp or an initial intake of the
breath of amazement

We're faced with a crystal glowing bright blue in a
dark forest whose trees seem to draw even closer to create a
kind of cloister in which to
view what goes on there in the crystal's
sky-like facets against night's velvety blackness

We're faced with a blank wall of
transparency upon which all this apparent
life is happily or tragically projected we're

faced with it and the curious choices we've
made that got us this far and which
don't seem like choices at all but more like
either the results of reckless abandon or else a kind of
timid progression from breath to
breath from day to day from dream to
grave and out again among the living to start all
over again and I don't mean the
transmigration of souls back again into
living bodies after death but that the

whole cosmos as it spirals upward through blinking
on-again off-again split-second momentary flow actually

starts from Eve and Adam in each

charged atom out into visible inwardness and in beyond

interiority to display the Lord's Glory openly

2

And if the windows rattle it's the ever-flexible
wind articulating God's words making
sentences of imprecation announcing a storm

Who has no lips so the world's His lips

And if a fly comes into the room and
zooms around like an erratic zeppelin looking for an
out it's a part of God's grammar attempting to
encompass the living enigma an annoyance an
intrusion disturbing our peace unsettling us
until we open a window or door to
let it out

Who has no lips so the world's His lips

The earth rumbling in deep rifts of rocks grinding each other's
surfaces volcanic bursts mudslides roaring like an
angered dragon onto a village below burying the
villagers faces and arms helpless
sweet God's Voice heard suddenly almost
direct in raw verbs and adjectives the unmistakable
sound of His Majesty throwing the jewels down from His
earthen caves onto eyes unaccustomed to such
immortal brilliance

Who has no lips so the world's His lips

And our blood beats
and the xylophones and harps of its
beats resound through our physical system
the heart clock insistent on keeping the
only slightly variable beat
whose floods of living glory spread a river of
light through our living bodies
like an oration on humility like a whispered
constant counsel by a close family member a
mother a father with tears in his or her eyes
who speaks directly to us

Who has no lips so the world

speaks His speeches directly to us

and the heart hears it for the heart that heard it spoke it

and a white bird from Paradise floats on the
buoyant updrafts of it

as earth's lips move sometimes slightly sometimes mightily

to articulate all of it

8/22

54 A VERY OLD TIGER

A very old tiger showed up to pose for the symbol of Ferocity
a very paunchy elephant lumbered in for the Strength & Reliability logo
the peacock that strutted in for the Versatility and Beauty shot was
tattered and a little one-might-say "moth-eaten"
some feathers bent some eyes a little blurry

They got together at the side away from the
cameras and sketchpads with the
grouchy and slightly skeletal lion (Majesty) and the
fox with mange (Slyness and Quick Thinking) so that
islands of its red fur were simply not there
and started complaining among themselves like the
old hands they were
chuckling deep in their throats now and then and rolling their
bloodshot eyes

"The old days are long gone
and so are the days of our youth"

Then the tiger was called

He lurched a little unsteadily at first
but finally strode forward with grizzled head high

straightened his coat-hanger shoulders whipped his
threadbare tail around once and struck as
tiger-like a pose as they were likely to get at this
late hour and so few tigers readily available

He lifted his lips a little to show off his yellowed teeth
bent his eyes forward in fierce focus
and gave us his most mask-like *Tyger Tyger Burning Bright* face
the earth-energy of tigerness and the sky-energy of
vastly more than tigerness fusing for a moment in truly
admirable ferocity

And all the
others slapped their paws and trumpeted their
trunks and shrieked their peacock shrieks in
cacophonic approval

slapped each other on their backs and roared with
lilting animal laughter

For no thing is of itself alone at last
but is an emblem of itself and something
always more than itself for which it stands

8/24

55 VASES FULL OF ROSES

Vases full of roses catch fire and the
flames make a crackling music
voices speak through enunciating syllables of love

Smoke across the glass tables of Aronica
on the balconies of Tuscan
in the valley of Maroo

We go on so little we go on so much
it's in the way we read things and what we
use for a gauge

such as whether we watch the blue-green
flames rise from the rose-heads or rush to
douse them not with tears of joy and redemption but
buckets of the waters of unnecessary fears

Meanwhile love's roses blaze and light up the most
inaccessible
deep corners of the night here in this valley

Smoke across the glass tables of Aronica
on the balconies of Tuscan
in the valley of Maroo

Where every artifice is peeled back revealing more
roses in vases with blue-green flames in tiers

going infinitely back and back and even further back
igniting the night

8/27

56 IF THERE WERE A CHAIR

If there were a chair I could sit in that would
transport me wholly and pure to your realm O Lord

but knocking bereft on Your door is the way Lord
and drinking from the waters that

trickle under your door
hot waters cold waters intertwined

O the faces of flowers are scrubbed like schoolchildren
and the things of this world are like open books waiting for their

first lessons to be repeated again until they're learned

If I could sit under a tree like the Buddha did
and all his streaming demons crash like surf against his rock

splattering into small drops
my open eye looking at You direct

Or if I could simply walk into Your Presence from the
state I am in and I don't mean Pennsylvania

The olive trees gnarly on the hillsides
each olive nothing by itself but leached and

pressed it becomes the savior of the world

8/30

57 THE MUSIC OF THE SOUL

The music of the soul is a very battered old
upright piano playing by itself out of tune at
the end of a paint-peeling boardwalk in the
rain

The music of the soul is a squeaky bicycle ridden by a
very old botanist on her way to an
outcrop of rare spring blossoms in the next valley just after
sunrise

The music of the soul is writing a poem called
the music of the soul without knowing where it's going
either to begin or to end since it actually began
long before that first line up there and will
end long after it's over

The music of the soul is many coyotes howling in the
moonlight in New Mexico against
silhouettes of pine trees

The music of the soul is this insistent
refrain like the anticipation of a letter of
love or love's forgiveness day after day no matter
how many times the mind tries to
forget all about it

The music of the soul is a thin layer of golden sunlight along the
new fawn's back as it lies
close to the warmth of its mother in a
soft nest of needles

The music of the soul is the hope beyond hope to
catch even a shred of it in flight like the
pollen from certain highly aromatic
flowers carried by extremely
conscientious bees across actual
miles of open terrain in Antarctica

The music of the soul that goes on long after we're
physically spent like old books removed from
public library shelves due to cracked bindings and fewer
borrowers though I'd like to think that in fact we'll go out
of here in a real jubilant music of the soul jamboree
on shafts of gorgeous lights in dazzling wheels accompanied by
singers from as far away as Timbuktu in exalted
harmonies and the world's revealed scriptures as if
walking through in their glorious raiment of original
inspiration nakedly singing God's fresh revelations

Flights of lyrebirds and egrets in loops
conch shells and orchids from Polynesian islands
polyphonically crossing sound and smell in the air

The wavering clear but spatially liberating
watery melodies of choruses of singers singing in giant
circles under crystal domes of variegated
sunlight both the earthly and heavenly
music of the soul that opens the soul's
doors from inside one after another in
smooth and precise succession until both

birth and death and all the exasperating
moments in between are deep chords held
down and released at the same time
on the original piano there at the end of the
boardwalk in the rain of the
endless and beginningless
music of the soul

that enraptures all of us at once
as well as the stars and all their
millions of miles of dark starlight

across universes known and unknown in the open
soul-music song-chambers of our hearts playing by themselves

standing upright through every calamity at the end of
this insubstantial but weatherbeaten boardwalk

in the rain

9/2

THE VILLAGERS ARE COMING IN

The villagers are coming in
to look at the man they found this morning in the
cornfield
his mouth all torn and his eyes wild

They look down at him as if down into a
prison pen
he's tied to the table with thong

Worlds come and go worlds lift and fade
clouds roll and unroll above terrain
blasted and chill
but it only takes one like our man here
to show us the ravages that can happen
and the cry that can come from far away

He was a baby once though his eyes tell differently
he might have been married he might have been sane
now he's a scarecrow with thoughts locked up
inside a head like pure marble
like lightning caught in a golf ball like a
history too horrible to tell

Did he fall out of the sky?
Is he one of us?
How did he get here? On all fours? In a
kite?
Is he even human all the way though? Did you check
his fingernails his gums his genitals?
Is that car wrecked out on Highway 20 his?
The one halfway up the tree with the
hood still steaming?

No that's the Robinson kid's
this is somebody else this is something like we've
never seen before this is nightmare country this is
a man from outer space in the
pants and jacket of a human being

But if they only knew
he was a conduit and a messenger who barely had
time to deliver his message before the sky
fell on him and the earth rose up against him

He held hot coals in his mouth
he ate serpents he scratched fire
he walked on wind-shoes he lived in an electric body
his organs were in flames his organs were
music

Light behind his eyes was his constant and
loyal companion
and now the townspeople look down at him
as if he were an animal from an earlier myth

He'll never walk out of here
he'll never say "*good morning*"
he'll never put on his hat at
first daylight or simply
saunter away whistling

He's stretched out on the table before you
like a memory of stallions

Put a sunflower at his feet

Give him room to die

9/4

59 POEM FOR MY FRIEND THE BLIND POET/ PHOTOGRAPHER

for Dan Simpson

"*I'm a louse*" shouted the farmer
and the lice all headed for home

"*I'm a mouse*" said the grand piano
and the mice all scurried under the concertgoers' shuffling feet

"*I'm a flame*" sang the contralto
and all down the street wicks on café tables flickered

"*I'm a storm*" whispered the window
and its willowy curtains shivered ominously

"*I'm a wheelbarrow*" declared the limousine
and it dumped its bloated contents onto the road

"*I'm a lover*" rang the bell in the chestnut tree
and its fruits all fell ringing merrily onto the ground

"*I'm a tree*" yawned the lion behind its bars
and the metal vertical rods all sprouted leaves

"*I'm a blue sky*" trilled the wren flying between wires
and its wings caught fire in a blaze of bright turquoise

"*I'm a light in the darkness*" murmured the tiniest spark
and a corner of the darkness lifted its edge to reveal its innermost heart

"*I'm nothing at all*" said the believer
and a world of divine activity rolled across the universe like an ocean
and drowned him completely

until he stood with his feet wet
in a land of uttermost dryness

and each step he took filled with bright water

like a light in darkness in a blue sky
through the trees like a lover in a wheelbarrow
blowing up a storm in a flame so bright
it lights up the lives of both mouse and louse
as they leap through the hay in a barn
shouting "*I'm strands of spun gold
not hay I'm ladders to heaven rung by rung
I'm the woven fibers of Paradise I'm the very
moustaches and beard-hairs of Job!*"

9/8

60 FROM THE VERY BOTTOM

From the very bottom of the deepest point of the sea
where even blackness is non-existent except by the
lamplights that move ghostly through the dark

and from the deepest point in the center of the Milky Way's
giant black hole where it's said the density is so great it doesn't
crush all matter but instead etherializes it under such atomic
pressure no space is allowed no time no breath no
being no non-being life or death-song even a sigh or an
inaudible catch in the throat of the dying or the look of the
already dead once the air has passed over them

From these two extremities comes the same thunderous boom of
love that suspends us all by our hearts like a
starry hammock between two trees
and sets us rocking gently back and forth as if from a
subtle tropical breeze except it's the godly pulse
the jump in the blood the warble in birdsong the
rhythm of the way clouds mass and unmass in earth's most
delicate atmosphere

And on the staves of this swinging all the
music of our voices is strung into melodious

words just as the foam of God's ocean is about to
drown them

Words in a hurry to be said which once said sail
as stately as ocean liners across
the heart's green endlessness

9/9

61 A LITTLE RAMSHACKLE SHACK

I

A little ramshackle shack on a hill
blown apart by the wind
door roof and walls lofted aloft and sent flying
no weightier than paper upon which is casually written
a name
twists in the air almost signals goodbye then
suddenly is gone only
bare hillside left behind
a goat now stands upon
two goats a small herd after the wind's died down
straggle along distractedly
chewing

Madame X is led out to the guillotine where a
head once encircled by ermine on a tall neck once
encircled by strings of pearls and glittering diamonds
rolls like a dark pearl into a basket its
eyes rolled heavenward its body relaxed
backward like a flung necklace onto a
marble tabletop in an
empty room after the
ball is over

2

Imagine the precise and daunting gears and
levers of the decree that led to all those innocent
people meeting death at the World Trade Center in
New York September 11, 2001
all the little accumulating gestures and maneuvers that
put them at their desks on schedule in time to die
the horrific fireball of the angel of death who may have
appeared to them all at the last as
cool refreshing waterfalls of light or open
delightful corridors leading to emerald green
gardens so bright with joy they forgot completely
how they got there

We all wonder how we'll die
hoping for a soft bed in a warmly lit room surrounded by
loved ones after a short and not too uncomfortable
illness a kind of light cough or a
stitch in the side and that's all
never imagining falling to the ground from 110 stories in the air
or twisted in molten steel like a tyrant's cage
in suffocating smoke

Unthinkable

The high school diplomas the happy
vacation moments in Cancun across a turquoise pool
the epiphanies while reading Moby Dick
the birthday banquets with long-lost relatives
the recent wedding or long-awaited love letter received

It's a lone figure in a woolen hat on a sheer white hillside
whose coat trails the ground and whose
footprints evaporate once the meeting's taken place

It's unfathomable and beyond any human
words devised to describe it
and for all those souls lost in the New York disaster
whose accidental but destined martyrdom is absolutely assured
(except ironically to the fanatically deluded
hell-bound perpetrators of the unthinkable
disaster itself)

there are coats of eiderdown so soft and pearls so ethereally gorgeous
so filled with subatomic music that pours out of
every gap in their weave to envelop the air in
ecstatic choir

And the divine shadow of Truth moves aside to let pour
a radiance so pure every moment set in motion in time

one step after another year after year that led to their
being there in the right place at the
supreme right time
suddenly becomes a series of perfect stepping stones like floating
lily pads over deep black water to a Paradise even our
most ornate imaginations cannot adequately imagine

3

People are very involved with having
faces and eyes and thoughts of their own and
smells in the odorous parts of their
bodies where the human anatomy dictates

They move with a certain self-consciousness which is sometimes
nonchalant and at other times unnatural
they can feel their spines hunched or vertically straight
and how their rib-cages make room for their
breathing

People are curious capsules of atmospheres and internal weathers
and at complete ease are either blessed with expansive
horizons or cursed with tics and foibles that
intensely constrain them

a consciousness that may include the Serengeti for example with
all its wild flora and fauna or the
bleached out and tattered prospect of simply
four walls a ceiling and a floor

Young ones often betray a jumpy and eager quality
old ones a sleepy and generally exhausted quality though they
may achieve beneficence from time to time as their
bones creak and their nerves ache

But each one is categorically a cosmos and has vivid
cosmological thinking and a deep appreciation of its consequences
and each one experiences the end of the
world when death appears like a
yawning sea to drown them in its
perpetuity

drawing back within it the
essence of their beauty

4

This is the music space
where music is most difficult
this place of joy and horror
sound of fuselage entering steel as if

slicing through butter

This is the silence out of which
all the thrilling chords emerge

This is the space of the silence of souls
at their moment of release

This is the air over a dewy wheat field
crackling like cellophane in the morning light

This is the music space
voices in a room of those
visible and those who are invisible

I think the music of the spheres
can be heard in this space

It's the sound of life
which takes place without echo
or is nothing but echo

And the original sound is the
sound of God alone audible to Himself
and we are the humming elements of that sound

This is the music space
we hear it this very moment

It's the sound of hooves
and nothing at all like the sound of hooves

It's the endlessly heaving ocean-sound
which turns out to be our blood beating
and the deep tidal push of our own heartbeats

Each whisper of love and fear and grief
rises in this music space

And one single note is enough to fill it

And silence itself is part of it

And the silence or the sound that follows it
is also part of it

9/15-16

ABOUT THE AUTHOR

Born in 1940 in Oakland, California, Daniel Abdal-Hayy Moore's first book of poems, *Dawn Visions*, was published by Lawrence Ferlinghetti of City Lights Books, San Francisco, in 1964, and the second in 1972, *Burnt Heart/Ode to the War Dead*. He created and directed *The Floating Lotus Magic Opera Company* in Berkeley, California in the late 60s, and presented two major productions, *The Walls Are Running Blood*, and *Bliss Apocalypse*. He became a Sufi Muslim in 1970, performed the Hajj in 1972, and lived and traveled throughout Morocco, Spain, Algeria and Nigeria, landing in California and publishing *The Desert is the Only Way Out*, and *Chronicles of Akhira* in the early 80s (Zilzal Press). Residing in Philadelphia since 1990, in 1996 he published *The Ramadan Sonnets* (Jusoor/City Lights), and in 2002, *The Blind Beekeeper* (Jusoor/Syracuse University Press). He has been the major editor for a number of works, including *The Burdah* of Shaykh Busiri, translated by Shaykh Hamza Yusuf, and the poetry of Palestinian poet, Mahmoud Darwish, translated by Munir Akash. He is also widely published on the worldwide web: *The American Muslim, DeenPort*, and his own website, among others: www.danielmoorepoetry.com. The Ecstatic Exchange Series is bringing out the extensive body of his works of poetry, beginning in 2005 with *Mars & Beyond, Laughing Buddha Weeping Sufi, Salt Prayers* and a revised edition of *Ramadan Sonnets*, and continuing in 2006 with *Psalms for the Brokenhearted, I Imagine a Lion, Coattails of the Saint, Love is a Letter Burning in a High Wind* and *Abdallah Jones and the Disappearing-Dust Caper*. In 2007, *The Flame of Transformation Turns to Light, Underwater Galaxies* and *The Music Space* have continued this publication project.

POETIC WORKS BY DANIEL ABDAL-HAYY MOORE

Published and Unpublished
(many to appear in *The Ecstatic Exchange* Series)

Dawn Visions (published by City Lights, 1964)

Burnt Heart/Ode to the War Dead (published by City Lights, 1972)

This Body of Black Light Gone Through the Diamond (printed by Fred Stone, Cambridge, Mass, 1965)

On The Streets at Night Alone (1965?)

All Hail the Surgical Lamp (1967)

States of Amazement (1970)

Abdullah Jones and the Disappearing-Dust Caper (published by The Ecstatic Exchange, Crescent Series, 2006)

The Chronicles of Akhira (1981) (published by Zilzal Press with Typoglyphs by Karl Kempton, 1986)

Mouloud (1984) (A Zilzal Press chapbook, 1995)

Man is the Crown of Creation (1984)

The Look of the Lion (The Parabolas of Sight) (1984)

The Desert is the Only Way Out (completed 4/21/84) (Zilzal Press chapbook, 1985)

Atomic Dance (1984) (am here books, 1988)

Outlandish Tales (1984)

Awake as Never Before (12/26/84) (Zilzal Press chapbook, 1993)

Glorious Intervals (1/1/85) (Zilzal Press chapbook, ?)

Long Days on Earth/Book I (1/28 – 8/30/85)

Long Days on Earth/Book II (Hayy Ibn Yaqzan)

Long Days on Earth/Book III (1/22/86)

Long Days on Earth/Book IV (1986)

The Ramadan Sonnets (Long Days on Earth/Book V) (5/9 – 6/11/86) (Published by Jusoor/ City Lights Books, 1996) (Republished as Ramadan Sonnets by The Ecstatic Exchange 2005)

Long Days on Earth/Book VI (6-8/30/86)

Holograms (9/4/86 – 3/26/87)

History of the World (The Epic of Man's Survival) (4/7 – 6/18/87)

Exploratory Odes (6/25 – 10/18/87)

The Man at the End of the World (11/11 – 12/10/87)

The Perfect Orchestra (3/30 – 7/25/88)

Fed from Underground Springs (7/30 – 11/23/88)

Ideas of the Heart (11/27/88 – 5/5/89)

New Poems (scattered poems, out of series, from 3/24 – 8/9/89)

Facing Mecca (5/16 – 11/11/89)

A Maddening Disregard for the Passage of Time (11/17/89 – 5/20/90)

The Heart Falls in Love with Visions of Perfection (6/15/90 – 6/2/91)

Like When You Wave at a Train and the Train Hoots Back at You (Farid's Book) (6/11 – 7/26/91)

Orpheus Meets Morpheus (8/1/91– 3/14/92)

The Puzzle (3/21/92 – 8/17/93)

The Greater Vehicle (10/17/93 – 4/30/94)

A Hundred Little 3-D Pictures (5/14/94 – 9/11/95)

The Angel Broadcast (9/29 – 12/17/95)

Mecca/Medina Time-Warp (12/19/95 – 1/6/96) (Published as a Zilzal Press chapbook, 1996)

Miracle Songs for the Millennium (1/20 – 10/16/96)

The Blind Beekeeper (11/15/96 – 5/30/97) (Published 2002 by Jusoor/Syracuse University Press)

Chants for the Beauty Feast (6/3 – 10/28/97)

Open Doors (10/29/97 – 5/23/98)

Salt Prayers (5/29 – 10/24/98) (Published by The Ecstatic Exchange, 2005)

Some (10/25/98 – 4/25/99)

Flight to Egypt (5/1 – 5/16/99)

I Imagine a Lion (5/21 – 11/15/99) (Published by The Ecstatic Exchange, 2006)

Millennial Prognostications (11/25/99 – 2/2/2000)

The Book of Infinite Beauty (2/4 – 10/8/2000)

Blood Songs (10/9/2000 – 4/3/2001)

The Music Space (4/10 – 9/16/2001) (Published by The Ecstatic Exchange, 2007)

Where Death Goes (9/20/2001 – 5/1/2002) (Published by The Ecstatic Exchange, 2007)

The Flame of Transformation Turns to Light (99 Ghazals Written in English) (5/14 – 8/21/2002) (Published by The Ecstatic Exchange, 2007)

Through Rose-Colored Glasses (7/22/2002 – 1/15/2003)

Psalms for the Broken-Hearted (1/22 – 5/25/2003) (Published by The Ecstatic Exchange, 2006)

Hoopoe's Argument (5/27 – 9/18/03)

Love is a Letter Burning in a High Wind (9/21 – 11/6/2003) (Published by The Ecstatic Exchange, 2006)

Laughing Buddha/Weeping Sufi (11/7/2003 – 1/10/2004) (Published by The Ecstatic Exchange, 2005)

Mars and Beyond (1/20 – 3/29/2004) (Published by The Ecstatic Exchange, 2005)

Underwater Galaxies (4/5 – 7/21/2004) (Published by The Ecstatic Exchange, 2007)

Cooked Oranges (7/23/2004 – 1/24/2005)

Holiday from the Perfect Crime (1/25 – 6/11/2005)

Stories Too Fiery to Sing Too Watery to Whisper (6/13 – 10/24/2005)

Coattails of the Saint (10/26/2005 – 5/10/2006) (Published by The Ecstatic Exchange, 2006)

In the Realm of Neither (5/14/2006 – 11/12/06)

Invention of the Wheel (11/13/06 –)

www.ingramcontent.com/pod-product-compliance
Lightning Source LLC
Chambersburg PA
CBHW020910090426
42736CB00008B/560